The Moose Cookbook

Over 100 Ways to Cook Your Moose

By
Colonel John J. Koneazny

**Illustrated by Michelle Lydon
and Cheryl Kobilis**

Cover by Connie Kennedy

Published by

GSPH GENERAL STORE
PUBLISHING HOUSE

499 O'Brien Road, Renfrew Ontario, Canada K7V 4A6
Telephone 1-800-465-6072 Fax (613) 432-7184

ISBN 1-896182-57-7
Printed and bound in Canada
Printing by Custom Printers of Renfrew Ltd.

Copyright © 1997
General Store Publishing House

Canadian Cataloguing in Publication Data

Koneazny, John J.
    The moose cookbook: over 100 ways to cook your moose

(A Taste of Canada series)
isbn 1-896182-57-7

    1. Cookery (Moose) I. Title. II. Series.
TX751.K65 1997   641.6'91   C97-900002-5

Ninth Edition

Introduction

It was about ten o'clock in the morning with the wind blowing almost 25 miles per hour. Every few minutes a snow squall would pass and make it impossible to look upwind. I was on top of a mountain above the tree line in western Newfoundland. I had on shorts and a t-shirt under long johns. The next layer was hunting pants and shirt, then a hooded sweat shirt under a rain suit, and I was still cold!

The moose came in from behind me, and I didn't see him 'til he came alongside about 150 yards to my left. He obviously didn't see me as he was looking to his left towards where Roy was posted. I quickly took aim with my 30-06 "Gamemaster" and dropped him with one shot. He never moved.

When I came up to my moose (a ten-pointer), I could not believe his size. He was as large as a horse, a big horse. This was my first moose, so I guess I was expecting something twice as large as a deer. I had shot almost 50 deer and antelope in my lifetime, but they were pygmies compared to this bull moose. Art, our guide, said I would get 450 pounds of meat. Talk about beginner's luck! I was two hours into my first day out, and I bagged the first moose in the camp! Talk about euphoria!

There were six of us hunting and by Wednesday we all had our moose and were heading back to

Massachusetts. Three of us decided to have our meat butchered professionally and dropped our moose off at a shop in southern Maine. We had seen the advertisement in one of the hunting newspapers that we picked up in Sidney.

Of all the game that I cut up in my lifetime I never became a butcher. Every deer that I cut up was different. Bending over the counter for hours on end would give me a backache, and I'd have to extend the job over several days. It was one of my most disliked jobs, I was glad to hire it out.

The butcher did an excellent job! The meat was all double wrapped and labeled. He followed my instructions to the letter. I was very happy that I went that route! He charged $120.00 for a 1,200-pound animal.

It is very important to double wrap the meat. Unless you have eight or ten mouths to feed, some of that meat is going to be in the freezer for a long time, and moose meat is so good that it's a crime to let any of it get freezer burn. Wrapped and quickly frozen moose meat will keep for over three years that I know of, and maybe longer. Remember, if the meat starts to get burn or lose its flavor, it is still good in soups and stews. Cook it with a sauce, marinate it, grind it and make a paté, but don't throw it away. If nothing else give it to those starving folks we hear so much about.

As there are just two of us at home, my wife Dottie and I, even though we do quite a bit of entertaining, I could see the meat lasting for several years.

We had just had our cookbook, *Only the Best* published by R. & E. Publishers of San Jose, CA and the sales were brisk. I thought that maybe a moose cookbook might be the next project. We tried the moose meat many different ways, and kept notes as we went along. I do almost all of the cooking in our household, and am considered an inventive cook. I can say without reservations that moose meat is the best meat that I have ever worked with. It's lean, it's tender and it's tasty. My hunting companions are just as enthusiastic about it as I am.

It is not the intent of this book to give detailed instructions on how to field dress, transport and butcher your animal. But I will briefly mention cooling and aging, two important elements in the preservation and taste of your game.

Cooling:

It is important to cool the meat as soon as possible. Don't stack the quarters on the way in from the field if you can help it. Hang them overnight in a cool place where the air can circulate freely. Air circulation is very important. If nighttime temperature is warmer than 40°F (4°C) the quarters should be skinned to aid cooling. Keep the meat protected from flies. Rubbing it with black pepper will help.

Aging:
Aging makes the meat tender and in my opinion the longer it's aged, the more tender it is. The wildlife department hunting guide for Newfoundland and Labrador advises aging the meat for three to five days outdoors or up to 14 days in a cooler. Remove as much of the fat and bone as possible.

Liver:
It is recommended that the liver and kidneys not be eaten because of the high content of cadmium. I have not included any recipes for liver or kidneys because of this. I am not sure just how dangerous this is, but why take chances. If you eat moose or caribou liver and are in good health, drop me a line and let me know. Thank you.

Many of the recipes here have been adopted from dishes made with other meats, and these recipes can be used for other big game such as caribou, elk and deer. The cooking time should be almost the same, but you should always test the meat when nearly cooked.

Sauces:
Starting on page 15, you will find a section on sauces that go well with game, or may be called for in a recipe. This is not an all-inclusive list, so you may have to go elsewhere if you can't find the particular one you are looking for.

Marinades:
In the marinade section, you will find recipes for both hot and cold marinades. Marinades impart flavor to meat and are also a good tenderizer.

Moose hunts:
In the rear of the book you will find a section where you can record your moose hunts. There are sections for expenses and hunting data. There is also a place to keep your freezer inventory.

Using this cookbook with other meat:
Of course, this cookbook can be used with other game such as venison, elk, caribou, and antelope. Many of the recipes can be used with beef, pork and lamb. Basically, there is not much difference in the cooking of meats, although one might want to cook pork a little longer to avoid the chance of trichinosis.

Improvising:

These recipes can be varied, and if you don't have a called-for ingredient try a substitution or maybe you can omit it altogether. Remember, tastes vary, and what may taste good to me might not be liked by you. If you see an item in a recipe that you don't like the taste of, don't put it in.

Abbreviations:

T = tablespoon
TT = to taste (season it so it tastes good to you)
qt. = U.S. quart (32 oz.)
lb. = pound (U.S.)
t = teaspoon
pt. = U.S. pint (16 oz.)
cup = 8 U.S. oz

Well, that's it! I hope you find some different ways to cook your moose that will become some of your favorites. If you have any recipes that you think I would like or any comment to make please drop me a line in care of the publisher.

May you all have a great life!

Jack Koneazny

Table of Contents

SOUPS... 1
    Stock.. 2
    Moose Consommé... 4
    Double Consommé... 4
    Consommé Madeira.. 5
    Consommé with Noodles............................. 5
    Consommé with Mushrooms...................... 5
    Jellied Wine Consommé............................... 5
    Borsch.. 7
    Pot-au-Feu... 8
    Crock Pot Moose Soup.................................. 9
    Great Southwestern Soup............................ 10
    Norwegian Vegetable Soup w/ Moose.............. 12
    Moose and Barley Soup................................ 13

SAUCES.. 15
    White Roux.. 17
    Blonde.. 17
    Brown Roux... 17
    Bechamel Sauce... 18
    Béarnaise Sauce.. 19
    Apricot Basting Sauce.................................. 20
    Barbecue Sauces... 21

Quick and Easy Barbecue Sauce 22
Beer Sauce 22
Drawn Butter Sauce 23
Cider and Raisin Sauce 24
Cranberry-Orange Sauce 24
Caper Sauce 25
The Colonel's Game Sauce 26
Cumberland Sauce 27
Curry Sauce 28
Dill Sauce 29
Glazes for Game 30
Horseradish Cream Dressing 31
Horseradish Sauce 31
Madeira Sauce 32
Moscovite Sauce 32
Mushroom Sauce 33
Poivrade Sauce 34
Red Wine Sauce 35
Romaine Sauce 35
Velouté Sauce 36

SAUSAGE MAKING 37
Making Moose Sausage 38
Breakfast Casserole 40
Sausage with Polenta 42
Moose Salami or Sausage 44
Four Star Gumbo 45

HOW TO CORN MOOSE MEAT 47
    Corned Moose & Cabbage 50
    Corned Moose & Parsnips 51

HOW TO CURE PASTRAMI 53
    Home Cured Pastrami 54
    Sauerbraten 56

GROUND MOOSE RECIPES 57
    Mexican Meatballs 58
    Mooseballs w/ Lemon Sauce 60
    Surf & Turf Pasta 61
    Stuffed Peppers 62
    Moose Meat Roll 63
    Curried Moose with Eggplant 65
    Moose Manicotti 66
    Moose Mincemeat 67
    Moose Chili Con Carne 68
    Moose-saka 70
    Fettucini Bolognese 72
    Spanish Rice 73
    Moose Meatballs with Prunes 74
    Mexicali Stuffed Peppers 75
    Cornish Pasty 76
    Moose, Beans & Bourbon 77
    Fayaway Meat Loaf 78
    Cranberry Meat Loaf 80

Meat Loaf in a Blanket... 81
French Canadian Moose Pie.................................. 83
Marina Cay Casserole... 84

MARINADES 85
Cooked Marinade... 87
Uncooked Marinades 88
Oriental Marinade.. 90
Caper Marinade.. 90
Low-Cal Marinade.. 91
West Texas Marinade... 91
Anisette Marinade.. 92

STEAKS & CHOPS.. 93
Moose Fondue 94
Marinated Moose Español..................................... 95
Steak Chevillot... 96
Roulades... 97
Scaloppini Marsala... 98
Stir-fried Moose & Mushrooms............................. 99
Sukiyaki... 101
Steak Diane.. 102
Zegreb Sirloin Steak... 104
Moose Chow Mein.. 105
Moose Chops Florentine.. 106
Easy Moose & Scalloped Potatoes......................... 107
Korean Moose-ke-Barbe.. 109

Jamaican Jerked Moose Chops 110
Tenderloin with Bourbon 111
Swiss Steak 112
Moose & Black Bean Salsa 113
Grilled Sirloin w/ Stilton & Wine 114
Moose Schnitzel 115
Schnitzel Holstein 115
Paprika Schnitzel 116

ROASTS, STEWS & CASSEROLES 117
Braised Moose w/ Sour Cream 118
Burmese Ginger Moose 120
Moose & Apple Stew 121
Moose Bourguignonne 122
Moose with English Walnuts 124
Moose with Noodles, Sheffield 125
Pot Roast with Prunes 126
Moose, Indonesian Style 127
Moose Stroganoff 128
Alaskan Chuck Roast 130
Moose-Ham Casserole 131
Sicilian Pot Roast 132
Roast Moose w/ Poivrade Sauce 133
Roast Moose w/ Pecans & Apples 134
Roast Saddle of Moose 135

RIBS & KEBABS 137
    Braised Short Ribs 138
    Moose Kebabs 139

ORGAN MEATS 141
    Boiled Moose Heart 142
    Rolled Moose Heart, Stuffed 143
    Tongue 144
    Sweet & Sour Tongue 144
    Tongue in Raisin Sauce 145

DESSERTS 147
    Chocolate Mousse (Moose) 148

APPENDIX 151
    Standard Measure Conversions 152
    Oven Temperatures 154
    Moose Hunt and Freezer Inventory 155

INDEX 158

SOUPS

Stock

When butchering your moose – save as many of the bones as you can. These are the heart of basic stock. The stock may be canned or frozen and kept for years. You can never have enough stock on hand. It may be used as a base for soups, stews, sauces, gravies, aspics and liquid in many dishes.

Some basics for making stock:

1. Don't use aluminum pots.
2. Use uncooked meat, bones and trimmings.
3. Use as much meat as bones.
4. When using a bouquet garni use fresh herbs if possible.
5. Cover ingredients **completely** with cold water when cooking.
6. Skim off the scum and fat while cooking.
7. Cool stock before refrigerating or freezing.

3 lbs.	**moose stew meat, cubed**
2 lbs.	**soup bones**

5 qts.	**water**
4	**green onions and tops**
1	**large onion, studded with cloves**
1	**celery stalk with leaves**
	bouquet garni*
2 T	**salt**

Bake meat and bones in a 400° oven for 1 hour or until well browned on both sides. Remove from pan and place in a large pot. Pour fat off of baking pan and deglaze with one cup of water. Add to pot. Add remaining ingredients. Cover and simmer for 4 hours, skimming scum occasionally. Remove meat and vegetables and strain through several layers of cheesecloth. Chill and remove any fat before using.

*Bouquet garni is a mixture of various herbs such as parsley, bay leaf, thyme and marjoram. Usually put in a cheesecloth bag and tied.

Variation

Several carrots may be added.

Moose Consommé

Combine 3 qts. of moose stock with $1^1/2$ lbs. of lean moose meat (use less desirable cuts), and the whites and shells of two eggs. Bring slowly to a boil stirring all the while. Reduce heat and simmer for about one hour. The solids will settle to the bottom of the pot. Ladle out and strain through several layers of cheesecloth. Salt and pepper TT.

Double Consommé

Take 2 qts. of consommé and reduce it by half over a high flame. Stir in 3 t brandy. Correct seasoning, and serve hot with a sprig of parsley.

Many Soups from Moose Consommé

Consommé is the base for many soups.

Consommé Madeira
Add a cup of Madeira wine to one cup of consommé. Bring to a boil and serve hot.

Consommé with Noodles
Add several cups Chinese noodles to 6 cups of consommé and boil until noodles are tender, about 3 to 5 minutes.

Consommé with Mushrooms
Add 3/4 lbs. of mushrooms to 1 qt. of moose consommé. Simmer for 20 minutes, add salt and paprika and a little sherry wine.

Jellied Wine Consommé
Stir 2 T of gelatin mixed with a little water into 4 cups of boiling Double Consommé. Add 1 t sugar and 1 cup of dry red wine. Add a little lemon juice and salt and pepper if needed. Chill the soup until it sets, whip it lightly with a fork and serve in cups with a

little chopped Vidalia onion and parsley. Great for a hot summer lunch.

Now you get the idea, there are as many ways to elaborate on consommé as there are cooks. You may add avocados and sour cream or tomatoes, or make a vegetable soup adding what you have in the house. Onion soup is made from stock as well as "Borsch", the Russian beet soup. Oxtail is another soup you can make with your stock.

Moose are the largest deer species in the world. Large bull moose can weigh over 1,350 pounds!

Borsch

2 cups	tomato juice
4 cups	shredded beets
8 cups	water
1	onion, chopped fine
6	eggs or Eggbeaters
1 lb.	moose meat, cut 3/4" cubes
2 T	lemon juice
1/2 cup	sugar
1/2 t	salt

Put meat, beets, tomato juice and onion in a kettle and simmer about 30 minutes. Add lemon juice, sugar and salt and cook 30 minutes longer. Beat the eggs and add the hot soup to them a little at a time, stirring constantly. Serve at once.

ABOUT 8 SERVINGS

Pot-au-Feu

3 lbs.	moose chuck or shoulder rolled and tied
6 qts.	cold water
2 T	salt
1 t	black pepper
3	leeks
2	carrots
1	parsnip
1	turnip
	bouquet garni
1	onion stuck with 3 cloves

Place meat in large pot with water and salt and pepper. Tie the leeks together. Add to the pot along with the other veggies. Simmer for at least 4 hours. Strain broth and add a little kitchen bouquet.

Place stale or toasted bread in soup bowls and pour bouillon over. Place meat and vegetables on a platter and serve with your favorite gravy.

Crock Pot Moose Soup

3 cups	chopped, cooked moose
3 stalks	celery, chopped
3	carrots, sliced
2	onions, chopped
1-16 oz.	can tomatoes (undrained)
1	package frozen mixed vegetables
1	packet chili seasoning mix
1-1/2 qts.	moose or beef stock
1/3 cup	butter or margarine
1/2 cup	flour

Combine all ingredients except the butter and flour. Cover and cook on low for 8-10 hours. One hour before serving turn the crock pot on high. Blend butter and flour until smooth and add slowly to the soup. Cook and stir until soup is thick. Serve with crusty French bread.

Great Southwestern Soup

The original version was made with venison.

1 lb.	moose top round
2 t	olive oil
3 cloves	garlic, chopped
1	large onion, chopped
12 cups	water
2	tomatoes, chopped
1/2 cup	fresh cilantro
4	carrots, sliced
2	zucchini, sliced
2	jalapeño peppers, chopped
3 ears	corn cut in several pieces
2 t	ground cumin
1 t	black pepper
	juice of 1 lemon
	salt TT

Cut the meat in 1-inch cubes and brown in the olive oil for about 10 minutes with the garlic and onion. Add the water and remaining ingredients and simmer for one hour.

4-6 SERVINGS

Variations

There are many variations of this soup. Beans or rice can be added, or it can be made very spicy by adding hot sauce or extra pepper.

"Don't boil him Mable, can't you see he's a Friar?"

Norwegian Vegetable Soup with Moose

3 lbs.	short ribs
1	small head cabbage
2	medium onions, chopped
3	large carrots, chopped
1	whole nutmeg*
2	beef bouillon cubes or stock
2 t	salt
1/4 t	pepper
2 qts.	boiling water
1/2 cup	chopped parsley
	horseradish sauce (see under sauces)

Put first 9 ingredients in pot and cook over low heat for about 1 hour or until the meat is tender. Remove meat to a serving dish and keep warm. Make horseradish sauce.

*Remove nutmeg before serving.

Serve soup and then the meat with the horseradish sauce.

Moose and Barley Soup

2 gals.	water
1	soup bone with some meat
1/2 cup	chopped celery tops
1 T	salt
1/2 t	pepper
1/2 cup	uncooked barley
3 cups	coarsely chopped cabbage
1 cup	sliced carrots
1 cup	sliced celery
2 cups	sliced parsnips
2 cups	sliced onions
1-12 oz.	can tomato paste

Put first five ingredients in a large pot and simmer 1-2 hours until meat comes easily from the bone. Remove bone from pot, then remove meat from bone and return meat to the pot. Give the bone to the hound. Stir in the barley and cook for 30 minutes. Add remaining ingredients. Correct seasoning and cook for another 30 minutes.

8-10 SERVINGS

SAUCES

SAUCES

Sauces

In this section I have included only sauces that I think can be used on moose and other game. Many of them are over and above recipes in this book. Most of them can be used with steaks, chops and roasts. Either cook the meat in them, brush them on while cooking, pour them on just before serving or serve in a sauce boat with the meat. These sauces will give you much more variety when cooking your moose.

White Roux

1/4 cup   **butter**
1/4 cup   **flour**

Melt butter over low heat. Add flour and stir until well blended and bubbling throughout.

Blonde

Cook Roux 15 minutes longer.

Brown Roux

1/4 cup   **butter**
5 T   **flour**

Melt butter and add flour. Cook over low heat stirring constantly until mixture is light brown.

Bechamel Sauce

2 T	chopped onion
1/4 cup	diced celery
1	small carrot, chopped
2 sprigs	parsley
1 sprig	thyme
1	small bay leaf
2 cups	stock
2 T	butter
2 T	flour
1/2 cup	cream
	salt and pepper to taste

Add veggies and herbs to stock and cook 20 minutes. Strain. Melt butter and blend in flour. Return strained stock to the roux slowly and cook for 10 minutes, stirring constantly until thickened. Add cream, salt and pepper and heat.

Béarnaise Sauce

4	egg yolks
1 cup	butter
1 T	lemon juice
2 T	chopped tarragon
2 T	chopped shallots*
1 T	tarragon vinegar
2 T	white wine
1/4 t	salt
	white pepper to taste

Combine vinegar, shallots and pepper in a sauce pan. Cook rapidly until almost all the liquid is gone. In a small sauce pan, heat butter until bubbling but not brown.

In an electric blender, put in yolks, lemon juice and salt. Flip on high, then off. Turn motor to high and slowly add hot butter. Add vinegar mixture and blend for 4 seconds.

*If you don't have any shallots you may use onions, but don't tell anyone I told you!

Apricot Basting Sauce

1 cup	**apricot preserves**
1-1/2 T	**fresh ginger root, grated**
1 T	**cider vinegar**
1/2 T	**spicy mustard**

Cook all ingredients until well mixed and preserves are melted.

Barbecue Sauces

There are as many barbecue sauces as there are "backyard chefs." I have listed below the main ingredients for making your own "house" sauce. Try to mix and match with the following:

1 cup	ketchup or tomato soup or sauce
2 T	mustard – dry, seeds, chinese, spicy or with horseradish
1/4 cup	vinegar – cider, red wine, tarragon, or rice
1-4 T	sugar – white, brown, honey, syrup or low-cal sweetener
1/3 cup	onion – minced, chopped, juice, powder or salt
1-4 cloves	garlic – minced, chopped, powder or salt
2 T – 1/2 cup	fat – butter, margarine or oil
TT	Spices – ginger, nutmeg, chili powder, paprika, etc.
TT	Salt – seasoned salt, soy sauce or bouillon
TT	Pepper – black, red, tabasco, tiger sauce, etc.
TT	Other – Worcestershire, A-1, fruit, wine, brandy, gin, bourbon or beer

Quick and Easy Barbecue Sauce

2-10 oz.	**bottles chili sauce**
1-1 lb.	**can cranberry sauce**

Mix and heat until smooth. Great on ribs!

Beer Sauce

2 T	**butter**
1 t	**sugar**
2 cups	**stock**
	grated rind of 1 lemon
1	**bay leaf**
2 cups	**dark beer or ale**

Melt butter in a sauce pan. Cook sugar in butter until caramelized. Add stock and other ingredients and bring to a boil. Correct seasoning.

Drawn Butter Sauce

3 T	**flour**
3 T	**melted butter**
1/4 t	**salt**
1/4 t	**white pepper**
1-1/2 cups	**hot water**
4 T	**butter**
1 t	**lemon juice**

Melt butter, blend in flour and salt and pepper. Stir in water and boil for 5 minutes. Mix in remaining butter a little at a time and add the lemon juice.

Mustard Sauce: to 1 cup of drawn butter sauce add 1 T of prepared mustard.

Cider and Raisin Sauce

2 cups	cider
1/2 cup	brown sugar
1 cup	golden raisins
1/2 t	ground cinnamon
1 t	freshly grated nutmeg
3 T	cornstarch

Bring cider, sugar and raisins to a simmer over low heat. Add cornstarch mixed in a little cold water. Stir a few minutes until sauce is thickened.

Cranberry-Orange Sauce

1 lb.	fresh cranberries
2 cups	sugar
1/2 cup	orange juice
	salt TT
1/2 cup	port wine

Combine all ingredients in a sauce pan. Bring to a boil. Reduce heat and cover. Cook until the skins pop. Serve hot or cold.

Caper Sauce

1/4 cup	butter
1/4 cup	flour
2 cups	moose or beef broth
3 T	capers

Melt butter in sauce pan. Add flour. Stir until blended smooth. Bring broth to a boil and add it all at once to the butter mixture. Stir vigorously. Cook for 15 minutes and add capers. Serve hot.

Caper Mustard Sauce: Add 1 T spicy mustard to the above sauce. Cook several minutes.

In the middle ages, moose were domesticated and used for pack animals.

The Colonel's Game Sauce

1-16 oz.	can tomato sauce
4 oz.	margarine or butter
1-12 oz.	bottle ale
2 oz.	Worcestershire sauce
10 oz.	ketchup
1 T	lemon juice
1 T	kitchen bouquet
1 T	sugar
1	large onion, minced
2 cloves	garlic, minced
2 T	spicy mustard
4 oz.	cream sherry

Combine all ingredients and simmer 10 to 15 minutes. Can be used as a basting sauce or served on or with the meat. Keeps well in the refrigerator.

Cumberland Sauce

1/4 pt.	**currant jelly**
1/4 pt.	**port wine**
	juice of an orange
	juice of a lemon
	pepper TT

Heat all ingredients in a sauce pan (do not boil) for about 15 minutes.

Curry Sauce

1-1/2 T	butter or margarine
1	onion minced
1 T	curry powder
1/2 t	brown sugar
2 T	flour
2 cups	moose or beef broth
2 cups	port wine

Melt butter in sauce pan and sauté onion until light brown. Add curry powder and sugar. Stir in flour and gradually add the liquids, stirring constantly. Cook for about 10 minutes. Correct seasoning.

Dill Sauce

1/4 cup	butter
1/4 cup	flour
1/4 t	pepper
2 cups	moose or beef stock
	salt TT
1-1/2 t	sugar
1 T	cider vinegar
1/4 cup	half and half cream
1/4 cup	chopped fresh dill

Melt butter in a sauce pan over medium heat. Mix in flour and pepper. Gradually add half the stock, stirring constantly. Blend. Stir in remaining stock and bring to a boil, stirring constantly. Reduce heat and simmer for 10 minutes. Add salt, sugar and vinegar. Add the cream slowly, stirring constantly. Stir in the dill and simmer 5 minutes longer.

Glazes for Game

To 1 cup of brown sauce add $1/2$ T gelatin softened in $1/4$ cup of water. Melt over hot water and apply to your moose.

Currant Glaze: Melt 1 jar currant jelly in a sauce pan. Brush over roasts.

Honey Glaze: Brush 1 cup of honey over roast.

Mustard Glaze: Mix a good mustard with a little brandy and brush over meat.

Tomato Glaze: Mix 1 cup of ketchup with 2 T Worcestershire sauce while cooking steaks and chops.

Horseradish Cream Dressing

1 cup	heavy cream
1 T	lemon juice
2 T	vinegar
1 t	tarragon
3 T	grated horseradish
	salt TT
	sugar TT
1/2 t	mustard

Whip cream. Add lemon juice and vinegar gradually and stir in seasonings. Serve with cold meats.

Horseradish Sauce

1-12 oz.	package cream cheese
1 cup	sour cream
1 t	onion powder
3 T	horseradish
1/4 t	sugar
	salt and pepper TT

Mix in blender. Serve with roast moose.

Madeira Sauce

Heat 2 cups Brown Roux (see page 17) until reduced by half. Add 1/2 cup Madeira wine. Heat but do not boil.

Moscovite Sauce

1 t	juniper berries
1/4 cup	water
1-1/2 cups	poivrade sauce (see page 34)
1 cup	seedless white grapes, halved
3 T	toasted almonds, chopped
3 T	raisins

Simmer juniper berries in water for about 15 minutes. Strain and add to the poivrade sauce. Add remaining ingredients and cook for a few minutes. Correct seasoning with salt and pepper.

Mushroom Sauce

2 T	**butter**
1/2 lb.	**mushrooms, sliced**
2 T	**flour**
1 cup	**moose broth (beef, chicken)**
1/4 t	**salt**
	pepper TT

Melt butter and add mushrooms. Cook for 5 minutes. Blend in flour and add broth gradually. Cook until thickened, stirring constantly. Add seasonings and serve hot alongside meat.

Poivrade Sauce

Poivrade sauce is especially good with game.

6 T	olive oil
1	carrot, diced
1	onion, diced
1/2 cup	flour
3 cups	brown stock
1 cup	tomato purée
4 sprigs	parsley
1/2 t	thyme
1	bay leaf
1/2 cup	moose or beef bouillon
1/2 cup	vinegar
6	peppercorns, crushed
1/2 cup	red wine

Heat oil in sauce pan. Add carrot and onion and cook until golden. Add stock and purée and cook until well blended. Add spices and cook over low heat for 1 1/2 hours, stirring and skimming as needed.

Put vinegar and bouillon in another pan and add peppercorns, then cook until reduced by two thirds. Strain the sauce into the vinegar mixture and cook another 30 minutes. Skim, add the wine and serve.

Red Wine Sauce

3	medium onions, chopped
1	green pepper, chopped
1 cup	celery, diced
1-1/2 cups	red wine
1 cup	tomato juice
	sugar and/or salt TT

Sauté the veggies in a little of the red wine until limp. Add remaining ingredients and cook for 15 minutes.

Romaine Sauce

2 T	sugar
1/2 cup	cider vinegar
1 cup	brown sauce
2 T	raisins

Cook sugar in sauce pan until light brown. Add vinegar and cook down to about 1 oz. Stir in brown sauce and bring to a boil. Add raisins and cook for about 10 minutes.

Velouté Sauce

2 T	butter
2 T	flour
1 cup	chicken or moose stock
1/4 t	salt
	few grains white pepper

Combine butter and flour, stir in stock slowly and heat to boiling. Cook until thickened, stirring often. Add salt and pepper.

SAUSAGE
MAKING

Making Moose Sausage

It's easier than you may think to make your own sausage. All that you need is a meat grinder or a food processor, some meat and spices.

With moose or any other game the scarcity of fat will make a very dry sausage so the fat of pork or beef should be added. If you are trying to lower your cholesterol, cut back on the fat. I once had a pork and apple sausage that was excellent and very low fat. I could never get the recipe, but it would be worth experimenting with. Maybe they used dried apples. If you do have a recipe for one that turns out well, please send me the recipe.

Penzeys Ltd., Spice House, P.O. Box 1448, Waukesha, Wisconsin, 53187 (phone (414) 574-0277) will send you their catalog which contains seasoning mixes for bratwurst, breakfast sausage, Italian, Polish, Russian, venison and pizza sausage.

2 lbs.	**trimmed moose meat**
1/2 lb.	**pork or beef fat**
1 t	**salt**
1/2 t	**garlic powder**
1/2 t	**fennel seed**

3/4 t	**ground pepper**
1 t	**sugar**
3/4 t	**paprika**
1/2 t	**ground celery seed**
1/4 t	**ground sage**
1 T	**soy sauce**
3/4 T	**Worcestershire sauce**

Mix all above ingredients with the meat, cover and refrigerate overnight. Grind it all and mix well. Fry out a small patty to check the taste. Correct seasoning if necessary. In order to make link sausage you will need a sausage stuffer or a feeding tube for your food processor and an extra set of hands.

When stuffing sausage keep the meat cold and it will work easier. Try different recipes and develop your own special "house" sausage.

The following can be used in your sausage: oregano, red pepper, basil, mustard, marjoram, mace, cinnamon, nutmeg and coriander.

Breakfast Casserole

This will serve a crowd when you don't feel like cooking to order for a mob.

2-1/2 cups	herb-seasoned croutons
2 cups	shredded sharp cheese
1 cup	sliced mushrooms
1 cup	peas, drained
1 cup	corn, drained
1/4 cup	green olives, chopped
2 lb.	moose sausage, bulk
1	large onion, chopped
12	eggs
2-1/2 cups	milk
1-10 oz.	can cream of mushroom soup
1 t	dry mustard
	tomato wedges
	snipped parsley

Preheat oven to 350° F. Grease 8x10 baking dish. Fry moose and onions and drain. Arrange croutons in bottom of the baking dish. Sprinkle on cheese and mushrooms. Next add the layer of sausage and onions. With a wire whisk lightly beat the eggs, milk, mustard and soup. Stir in olives, corn and peas and pour over ingredients in the casserole. Bake until firm throughout (test with a straw).

8-10 SERVINGS

"I don't care if your feet are cold, moose are supposed to stand in water!"

Sausage with Polenta

1 lb.	moose sausages
1	medium onion, chopped
1-2 cloves	garlic, minced
1	small can mushrooms
1 cup	tomato sauce
1 t	sugar
1 cup	canned tomatoes
4 cups	hot polenta
	salt and pepper TT
4-8 T	grated cheese

Cut sausage into serving size pieces and fry until brown. Add the onion and garlic and brown lightly. Add mushrooms, tomatoes and tomato sauce. Cover and simmer 40-50 minutes. Correct seasoning and add sugar.

Meanwhile, make polenta:
Bring 2^1/2 cups water to a boil with 1 T salt. Mix 1 cup white cornmeal with 1^1/2 cups cold water, add to boiling water and stir until it comes to a boil. Place over flame tamer or very low heat and cook 45 minutes, stirring occasionally. This will make 4 cups.

Spread polenta on a platter and cover with the sauce. Sprinkle cheese on top and surround with sausages.

4-6 SERVINGS

Variations

1. Add 1/2 lb. cubed mozzarella cheese to corn meal while cooking.
2. Add a little sage and/or oregano to the sauce.
3. Use fresh mushrooms instead of canned.

Approximately 3% of all bull moose die each year from wounds caused by fighting other bull moose.

Moose Salami or Sausage

This receipe is from the kitchen of Dona Wall, from North Bay, Ontario.

7 lbs.	**moose meat**
3 lbs.	**pork**
12 oz.	**commercial spice mix***
1 pint	**water**
	hog or sheep casings

Mix meat, spice mix and water thoroughly in a tub. The mixture will be quite mushy. Stuff into hog casing for regular sausage or sheep casing for breakfast sausage. One bundle of hog casing will do about 80 lbs. of sausage. Keep the casing in water until using to avoid drying and tearing.

Smoking time depends on the type of smoker used and how dry you like your sausage. A good rule of thumb is to use a meat thermometer and bring the internal meat temperature up to 170°. Your sausage will be ready to eat at this temperature.

*Available at Penzeys Ltd., P.O. Box 1448, Waukesha, WI USA 53187.

Four Star Gumbo

Here's a real great gumbo for your most honored guests. This is my recipe that has appeared in *Georgia Fishing World, Cruising World, People and Food,* and *Only the Best.*

3-1/2 cups	canned tomatoes
2 cups	tomato juice
4 cups	water
10	bay leaves
	salt and pepper TT
1 lb.	fresh okra
4 strips	bacon
1/2 lb.	moose meat, cubed
1/2 lb.	smoked sausage, cut 1"
4 T	flour
2	large onions, chopped
2 cloves	garlic, minced
2 cups	cooked shelled shrimp
1 T	gumbo filé
4-6 cups	hot boiled rice

Combine tomatoes, juice, water and seasonings in a large kettle. In a fry pan, fry bacon until crisp, add moose and sausage and brown. Add flour, onions and garlic and cook until flour is brown. Add to the kettle, then add shrimp and okra. Simmer for 1½ hours. Add filé and serve on mounds of hot rice in deep soup dishes.

8-10 SERVINGS

HOW TO CORN MOOSE MEAT

How to Corn Moose Meat

Before the invention of refrigeration, corning was a necessity, but today most of the people who live near civilization corn meat mostly for the taste. And what would we do without corned beef and cabbage on St. Patrick's Day?

Moose brisket, flank meat or other tough cuts may be used. One word of caution: Be sure to use salt without any iodine or free flowing agent. Kosher or pickling salts are a good choice.

Tenderizing salt is a mixture of sugar, salt and preservatives, and can be purchased in most specialty markets.

2-3 lbs.	moose brisket, etc. about 1 inch thick
1/2 gal.	distilled water
1/2 cup	kosher salt
1/2 cup	tenderizing salt
4 T	sugar
3	bay leafs
2 T	pickling spices
1 t	freshly grated black pepper
1-4 cloves	garlic, chopped

Roll brisket and tie. Put in a small crock or a glass bowl. Bring the remaining ingredients to a boil. Cool and pour over meat. Cover meat with liquid. Cover with plastic wrap and refrigerate for at least 5 days.

Corned Moose and Cabbage

3 lbs.	corned moose
8	peppercorns
1 clove	garlic
8	large carrots
8	small onions
1 head	cabbage, quartered
4 stalks	celery

Put meat in a large pot with peppercorns and garlic and cover with water. Simmer meat for 2-3 hours, until tender. Remove meat from pot. Peel and cut up vegetables and cook in the corned moose water until done. Reheat the meat in the water. Drain and serve.

6-8 SERVINGS

Variation

Turnips, winter squash or parsnips can be used in place of or in addition to the above.

Corned Moose and Parsnips

3 cups	**mashed, cooked parsnips**
	salt and pepper TT
1-1/2 cups	**corned moose cooked**
1 cup	**canned mushrooms**
1 cup	**grated cheese**
1/4 cup	**dry white wine**
	seasoned bread crumbs

Season parsnips with salt and pepper. Cube meat and mix with mushrooms, cheese and wine. Put alternate layers of meat and parsnips in a greased two-quart casserole. Cover with the crumbs. Bake in a 350° oven for 25 to 30 minutes.

4 SERVINGS

HOW TO CURE PASTRAMI

Home Cured Pastrami

You need a home smoker to make your own pastrami.

1-4-5 lb.	**slab of moose flank (brisket may be used)**
1/2 cup	**kosher salt**
2 T	**sugar**
2 t	**ground ginger**
1 t	**saltpeter***
1 T	**coriander seed**
1/4 cup	**peppercorns**
2 cloves	**garlic, chopped**

*Try your local drug store.

Combine the salt, sugar, ginger and saltpeter in a bowl. Crush the coriander and pepper and add to the mixture. Rub the mixture into the meat, put the meat in a plastic bag and seal. Put the plastic bag in the refrigerator for 8 to 10 days, turning the bag over once a day.

Drain the liquid from the meat, saving the solids, which should be rubbed back into the meat. Run some string through the meat with a large needle, hang and let dry in a cool place for 24 hours. Use an electric fan to assist the drying, or hang outdoors in the wind.

Put the meat in a smoker for about 3 hours at 150°. When ready to eat, cover with water and simmer for a couple of hours until tender.

Serve on rye or pumpernickel bread with vidalia onions and spicy mustard.

10 SERVINGS

Sauerbraten

If you have a tough chunk of moose meat, here is an old German way to make it tender:

2-3 lb.	moose shoulder
2-3 cloves	garlic, sliced
2 cups	vinegar
2 cups	white wine
3	large onions, sliced
2	bay leaves
1 t	peppercorns
1/4 cup	brown sugar
	oil for browning
	flour or corn starch
1 cup	sour cream

Put meat, garlic, and peppercorns in a glass bowl. Heat vinegar, wine, onions and sugar but do not boil. Pour over meat and cover bowl. Let stand in a cool place (refrigerator) for a week, turning every day. Remove meat, saving liquid and brown in hot oil. Add half the marinade, cover and simmer for several hours until tender. Add more marinade if needed. Remove meat and strain liquid. Reheat liquid and thicken with flour or cornstarch. Add sour cream and serve with buttered poppy seed noodles.

6 SERVINGS

GROUND MOOSE RECIPES

Mexican Meatballs

SAUCE

1 clove	garlic, crushed
1/4 cup	olive oil
1 cup	rich tomato sauce
2 cups	beef broth
	salt and pepper TT
3/4 t	oregano
1/8 t	cumin
2	chilies*

MEATBALLS

2 lbs.	moose hamburger
1/8 cup	minced onion
2 slices	dry bread or seasoned breadcrumbs
1/4 cup	milk
2	eggs
2-4 t	chili power TT

* May be omitted for ulcer patients, kids and sissies.

SAUCE:
Sauté onion and garlic in oil. Add remaining ingredients listed under sauce. Bring to a boil then lower heat to simmer.

Meatballs:
Combine hamburg, onion, bread, milk and beaten eggs. Add salt, pepper and chili powder. Make 1-inch meatballs. Bake on cookie sheets at 350° about 30 minutes. Add to hot sauce in chaffing dish and eat with party picks. Better if made the day before and marinated in the sauce.

Mooseballs w/ Lemon Sauce

2 lbs.	moose hamburger
1	large onion minced
3 T	chopped mint leaves
3 T	chopped parsley
1/8 cup	long grain rice
	salt and pepper TT
1 clove	garlic, pressed
4 T	A-1 sauce
1/8 t	coriander
1/8 cup	flour
2 cups	water, or stock or bouillon
2 T	butter or margarine
	juice of two lemons
2	eggs, separated

Mix hamburg and next 9 ingredients and make into 1-inch meatlballs. Boil broth or water, add butter and meatballs. Simmer covered for about 40 minutes. Pour stock into bowl. Add lemon juice. Beat egg yolks until frothy. Beat whites to peaks. Fold into yolks. In a thin stream pour stock into eggs. Pour over meatballs.

6 SERVINGS

Surf and Turf Pasta

1 lb.	moose hamburg
3	onions, chopped
1-16 oz.	jar spaghetti sauce
1-10 oz.	can whole baby clams
4 oz.	mushrooms, sliced
1 t	tarragon
1 t	basil
1 t	thyme
1 t	oregano
2 T	A-1 sauce
	seasoned salt and pepper TT

Brown hamburg and onions in a little oil or lo-cal spray. Add remaining ingredients and simmer about 20 minutes. Correct seasoning and serve over hot noodles.

Stuffed Peppers

2 T	cooking oil
1 lb.	moose hamburg
2 cups	cooked rice
1/4 cup	chopped onions
1/4 cup	chopped pimentos
1/4 cup	chopped green olives
4	large green peppers, sliced in half lengthwise
	salt and pepper TT
	white wine
	bread crumbs

Sauté hamburg in oil, add onions, pimentos and olives. Add rice and seasoning. Cook 5-10 minutes and add wine to make the mixture quite moist. Boil or steam peppers for a few minutes. Place pepper halves in a baking dish that has been lightly oiled and put stuffing in the peppers. Sprinkle with crumbs and bake in a 350° oven for 30 minutes or until bubbling.

8 SERVINGS ●

Variations
1. Spice them up by adding hot sauce or chopped hot peppers.
2. Add chopped mushrooms.

Moose Meat Roll

2	beaten eggs
1/2 cup	tomato juice
3/4 cup	soft bread crumbs
1/4 t	ground cumin
1/2 t	oregano
	salt and pepper TT
2 cloves	garlic, chopped fine
1-1/2 lbs.	ground moose meat
1/2 lb.	ground pork
4 to 6 oz.	thinly sliced ham
6 slices	swiss cheese

Combine eggs and tomato juice in a bowl. Stir in the next five ingredients. Add the meat and mix. On waxed paper pat meat to an 8 x 10 inch rectangle. Place ham slices on top, leaving a small margin around the edge. Chop 4 slices of the cheese and sprinkle over the ham. Roll up the meat into a loaf using the waxed paper to lift. Place in an oven-proof dish or pan and bake at 350° for 1 hour. Place remaining cheese on top of the loaf and return to the oven for a few minutes until cheese is melted.

8 SERVINGS

Variations

1. For a spicier loaf, add 2 T mustard, 2 T ketchup and A-1 sauce TT.
2. Add curry powder or chili powder for more zest.

"Look Mervin, I'm going to stay down here in Florida 'til the hunting season is over. Have you heard about that new cookbook with nothing but moose recipes?"

Curried Moose with Eggplant

2	medium onions, chopped
1 lb.	moose sirloin cut in 1" cubes or 1 lb. moose hamburg
2 or 3 t	instant beef bouillon
1	large eggplant, peeled and cubed
1 can	nacho cheese soup (Campbell's)
1/2 cup	golden raisins
5 oz.	cream sherry
1 t	curry powder
	salt and pepper TT
	water
3 T	olive oil

Use an electric fry pan if you have one, otherwise a large fry pan or pot will do. Put oil in pan, add onions, cook a few minutes then add meat and bouillon and brown. Add eggplant and cook for a few minutes then add soup, wine, raisins and curry powder. Cover and cook until eggplant is done. Add water if needed while cooking. Correct seasoning. This will be a little spicy hot. If you have ulcers or a tender mouth use cheddar cheese soup in place of the nacho cheese.

4-6 SERVINGS

Moose Manicotti

1/2 lb.	moose hamburg
1-16 oz.	jar of spaghetti sauce
2 oz.	dry white wine
2 cups	shredded mozzarella cheese
1 cup	ricotta cheese
1/2 cup	grated parmesan cheese
2	large eggs, beaten
1/4 cup	snipped parsley
1/2 t	salt
8	manicotti shells, cooked and drained (don't over cook!)

Sauté hamburg in a little olive oil. Add spaghetti sauce and wine. Simmer about 15 minutes. Meanwhile, combine 1 cup mozzarella, the ricotta cheese and the parmesan. Add eggs, parsley and salt. Mix lightly and stuff the shells. Pour enough of the sauce in a 2 qt. baking dish to cover the bottom. Put shells in dish and pour the remaining sauce over. Sprinkle with the remaining cheese and bake uncovered in a 350° oven for about 30 minutes or until bubbly.

4 SERVINGS

Moose Mincemeat

2 lbs.	moose hamburger or stew meat, diced
1 lb.	suet
1 lb.	sugar or honey
1 lb.	raisins
1 lb.	currants
2 lbs.	apples, peeled, cored, sliced
1/4 lb.	citron
1/4 lb.	candied lemon peel
	grated rind of 1/2 lemon
	grated rind of 1 orange
1	nutmeg grated
1/2 T	ground cloves
1/2 T	ground cinnamon
1/2 t	salt
1/4 cup	orange juice
1/4 cup	lemon juice
4 cups	cider
4 cups	brandy

Boil meat until tender. Drain and cool. Run through a food processor or meat grinder. Combine all ingredients except brandy and slowly cook about 1 1/2 hours. Remove from heat, add brandy and put in sterile jars at once. It will be ready in a week, and will keep indefinitely.

MAKES ABOUT 6 QUARTS

Moose Chili Con Carne

1 lb.	moose hamburg or steak cut in 1" cubes
1 lb.	onions, sliced
1 t	beef bouillon
3 cloves	garlic, minced
1 or 2	1 lb. cans kidney beans, drained and rinsed
1	10 oz. can tomato sauce
	chili powder TT
1 T	sugar
	red wine
	hot sauce

Sauté meat and onions with spices in a large frying pan until meat is brown and onions are soft. Add remaining ingredients and simmer 30 minutes, a little longer if using tougher chunks. Correct seasoning.

3-6 SERVINGS

Moose-saka

This near-Eastern dish is made with lamb, but if moose grew in those parts I bet they would forget about the traditional lamb in a hurry!

1	large eggplant, peeled
1/4 cup	flour
	salt and pepper TT
1/8 cup	olive oil
1 lb.	moose hamburg
1 cup	chopped onions
1 lb.	can tomato sauce
1 small can	tomato paste
1 cup	white wine
1/2 cup	water
2 cups	bread crumbs
3/4–1 cup	grated parmesan cheese
1/4 T	butter or margarine
1 t	oregano

Slice eggplant, coat with seasoned flour and fry in hot oil until brown and soft. Drain and keep warm. Brown meat, add onion, and cook until limp. Stir in tomato sauce and paste, wine, water and spices. Cook for about 15 minutes or until sauce is slightly thickened. Layer sauce, eggplant, sauce, eggplant, sauce in a 9x12" baking dish, sprinkling grated cheese on each layer and on top. Cover with crumbs, dot with butter, cover with foil and bake in a 350° oven for about 55 minutes or until bubbling in the center.

6 SERVINGS

Variations

1. In Greece they line the pan with sliced potatoes. I prefer the mousaka without.
2. Sprinkle crumbled feta cheese throughout the dish.
3. Add rosemary, thyme, tarragon or all three to the sauce.
4. Put a little sour cream between the layers.

Fettucini Bolognese

1 lb.	moose hamburg
1-1/2 cups	sliced mushrooms
1	small onion, chopped
1 clove	garlic, minced
12 oz.	tomato sauce
	red wine
4-6 oz.	cooked peas
chopped fresh basil or 1 t dried	
	salt and pepper TT
8 oz.	fettucini pasta

Brown hamburg, mushrooms, onion and garlic. Add a little wine and tomato sauce. Simmer for 20 minutes then add peas and simmer a few minutes more. Boil fettucini, drain and mix with sauce. Serve with a garden salad and warm Italian bread.

4 SERVINGS

Variations
1. Any other type of pasta or noodles can be used.
2. Add 1 t oregano.
3. $1/4$ cup sliced black olives may be added to the sauce.

Spanish Rice

6	slices bacon, chopped
1	onion, chopped
1	green pepper, chopped
1-1/2 lbs.	moose hamburg
1 t	instant beef bouillon
1 cup	uncooked Uncle Ben's rice
3-4 cups	tomato juice
1 t	paprika
1 t	Worcestershire sauce
1/8 t	saffron (optional)

Sauté or nuke bacon. Pour off most of fat and brown onion, hamburg and bouillon. Add rice to pan and sauté for several minutes. Heat tomato juice with remaining ingredients and add 2 cups to moose mixture. Pour into a greased casserole and bake in a 350° oven for about 30 minutes or until rice is tender. Add more tomato juice as it is absorbed.

6 SERVINGS

Moose Meatballs with Prunes

2 lbs.	moose hamburg
1/2 lb.	pork sausage
15	pitted prunes
1-1/2 cups	bread crumbs
1/2 cup	milk
2 T	soy sauce
	pepper TT
1	egg
2 oz.	dry red wine
6 oz.	ketchup
2 T	spicy mustard
4 oz.	water

Put prunes through a grinder or a food processor and mix with meat, crumbs, milk, spices and egg. Make the meatballs the size you desire. Make the sauce by combining the wine, ketchup, mustard and water.

Put meatballs in a greased pan and cover with the sauce. Bake in the oven at 350° for almost 1 hour. Turn occasionally. Serve warm at your next party with toothpicks as servers.

Mexicali Stuffed Peppers

1 lb.	moose hamburg
1 T	instant beef bouillon
1	large onion, chopped small
1-1 lb.	can corn
6	large peppers, ready for stuffing
2 T	cooking oil
12 oz.	tomato sauce or salsa
2 T	chili powder or TT
1/2 t	cumin
	hot sauce TT

Heat oil and fry onion and moose adding bouillon and cook until brown. Add corn and spices and cook several minutes. Add tomato sauce. Stuff peppers and pour any extra sauce over. Cover and heat in a 375° oven about 40 minutes, or microwave 12-16 minutes.

6 SERVINGS

Cornish Pasty

These little pies were made by the wives of Cornish tin miners to put in their lunch boxes. There are many fillings, but most of them have meat, potatoes and vegetables in a rich thick gravy. The ones I have had on the upper peninsula of Michigan were filled with hash. Almost every country has their own version of meat mixtures wrapped in dough. Moose and apple stew would make a good stuffing. The Cornish women sometimes made an extra compartment and stuffed it with apples or other fruit for dessert.

Roll out some pie dough in an 8- or 9-inch circle. Put the stew or other filling in the center of the dough. Fold over and seal around the edge with a fork. Brush with beaten egg and bake in a quick oven until golden. If you put in the dessert, seal between the stew and pie.

Moose, Beans and Bourbon

This dish can be cooked the old slow cook way or use the canned beans to speed up the cooking process.

3-1 lb.	cans baked beans
1 lb.	moose hamburg
1	large onion, chopped
4-5 T	spicy mustard
1 cup	ketchup
4 T	honey
1/4 cup	bourbon

Fry out the hamburg in bacon fat and put in a large pot. Add canned beans and all other ingredients except the bourbon. Cook over low heat for about 30 minutes. Correct seasoning and add bourbon.

6-8 SERVINGS

Variation

Chop up some bacon, salt pork or little sausages and fry out before you add the hamburg.

77

Fayaway Meat Loaf

1 lb.	moose hamburger
1 cup	onion, chopped
8-10	black olives, chopped
3 T	mustard
1/2 cup	ketchup
1/2 t	each of basil, marjoram, and tarragon
2	eggs, lightly beaten
2 oz.	grated cheese
2 T	Worcestershire sauce
2 T	steak sauce
4 T	cream sherry
	seasoned bread crumbs
	tomato and cheese slices

Mix all ingredients well except crumbs, tomato and cheese slices. Add enough crumbs to dry the mixture some. Form into a loaf in a loaf pan. Place tomato and cheese slices on top (make a design) and bake in a 350° oven one hour. Serve with baked potatoes.

6 SERVINGS

Variations

1. Add 4 or 5 T cottage cheese.
2. Add 3 T horseradish.
3. Omit ketchup and wine and add a can of cream of mushroom soup.

Cranberry Meat Loaf

1/4 cup	brown sugar
1/2 cup	cranberry sauce
1-1/2 lbs.	moose hamburg
1/2 lb.	ground smoked ham
3/4 cup	milk
2	eggs
3/4 cup	cracker crumbs
1-1/2 t	salt or instant beef bouillon
1/4 t	pepper
4 T	diced onion
3 strips	bacon

Spread sugar over bottom of greased loaf pan. Mash cranberry sauce and spread over sugar. Combine remaining ingredients except bacon. Shape into a loaf and place on top of the cranberry sauce. Put bacon on top of the loaf and bake in a 350° oven about 1 hour.

12 SERVINGS

Meat Loaf in a Blanket

1	onion, chopped
	cooking oil or spray
2 cups	finely chopped cooked potatoes
1-1/2 lbs.	moose hamburg
1 T	instant beef bouillon
1 T	mustard
1 T	Worcestershire sauce
1 t	paprika
3 T	tomato paste
2	eggs, lightly beaten
4 oz.	cheddar cheese, shredded
1 t	nutmeg
2 oz.	cream sherry
	biscuit dough (made with 2 cups of flour)

Brown meat and onions in oil. Add bouillon, mustard, Worcestershire, paprika and tomato sauce. Add potatoes and heat all together. Turn off heat and add all other ingredients except dough. Mix well and form into a loaf. Keep warm. Roll dough into a rectangle 1/4" thick. Place meat loaf in middle of the dough and draw up over the meat. Press edges of the dough firmly together. Slash top, put on a baking sheet and bake in a hot oven (425°) about 20 minutes. Serve with a mushroom sauce.

8 SERVINGS

"I told you Art, we should have brought the truck!"

French Canadian Moose Pie

1 clove	garlic
1 t	salt or instant bouillon
	pepper TT
1/2 t	nutmeg
1/8 t	mace
1	onion, minced
1 T	cornstarch
1 cup	liquid, 6 oz. water and 2 oz. red wine
1 lb.	moose hamburg
	pastry for a 2 crust pie

Mash garlic with salt or bouillon and mix in seasonings and cornstarch. Add liquid and blend. Put meat in a heavy saucepan and add mixture. Heat to boiling, then cover and simmer for 30 minutes. Line an 8-inch pie plate with pastry. Pour in meat mixture and put the top crust on, cut several slits for steam vents and bake in a 425° oven for about 30 minutes. Serve with candied sweet potatoes and a green "veggie."

6 SERVINGS

Marina Cay Casserole

1 lb.	moose hamburg
1/2 lb.	pork sausage
4	medium onions, chopped
1 clove	garlic, crushed
3 T	cooking oil
1 can	(1lb. 12 oz.) tomatoes
1-6 oz.	can tomato paste
1 can	french style green beans
1 cup	red wine
1/2 cup	sliced stuffed green olives
2 T	capers
1-1/2 t	salt
1/4 t	pepper
4	ripe plantains or bananas
2 oz.	oil to fry plantains
4	eggs

In a large saucepan fry meat, onions and garlic in oil. Add the next 8 ingredients and cook for 10 minutes. Meanwhile, peel plantains, slice lengthwise into 4 strips. Fry in hot oil until tender and brown. Drain on a paper towel. In a 3 qt. casserole, layer meat sauce and plantains alternately. End with meat sauce. Beat eggs and pour over meat. Bake at 350° for 45 minutes or until cooked throughout.

8 SERVINGS

MARINADES

Marinades

Marinating meat is especially important for tough game. Not only does it get moisture deep into the meat, but it also has a tenderizing effect. Steaks and chops should be marinated a couple of hours while roasts are best left in the marinade overnight, or better yet, two or three days. If you have a real tough piece of meat leave it for a week in the refrigerator. Turn it every day. Dry the meat well before you brown it. Always use a glass, enamel or earthware bowl when marinating. Some recipes call for using the marinade as the base for the sauce. In those cases use an uncooked marinade.

Cooked Marinade

3 cup	water
1 cup	dry white wine
1 cup	vinegar
2	onions, chopped
2 cloves	garlic, sliced
2	carrots, sliced
1 t	thyme
2	bay leaves
12	peppercorns
1 T	salt

Put the above ingredients in a pot and bring to a boil. Simmer for 45 minutes. Cool before pouring over the meat.

Uncooked Marinades

#1

1	**bay leaf**
1/4 t	**thyme**
1 t	**basil**
1 t	**salt**
10	**peppercorns**
2 T	**salad oil**
1 cup	**white or rosé wine**

Add meat and marinate in the refrigerator.

#2

2 cups	**red wine**
1 cup	**water**
1/4 t	**sage**
6	**cracked peppercorns**
1/2 t	**salt**

Use as above.

#3

4 oz.	salad oil
1 cup	dry vermouth
1/2 cup	brandy
1	lemon sliced thin
1/2 t	rosemary
2 cups	water

This marinade tends to separate so stir it frequently.

#4

1/2 cup	wine vinegar
2 cups	cool water
1 cup	dry red wine
3 T	lemon juice
3 T	orange juice
12	peppercorns ground
6	whole cloves
1/4 t	mustard seed
1 t	salt

Oriental Marinade

1/4 cup	soy sauce
1/4 cup	rice wine vinegar
1/4 cup	dry sherry
1/4 cup	lemon juice
1/4 cup	honey
1 t	sesame oil
1/2 t	five spice powder
1/2 t	garlic powder

Mix all ingredients in a blender.

Caper Marinade

1/2 cup	cider vinegar
1/4 cup	olive oil
2 T	capers
1/4 cup	cream sherry
2 T	spicy mustard
	salt TT
	pepper TT

Marinate roasts overnight.

Low-Cal Marinade

6 oz.	unsweetened pineapple juice
1/4 cup	soy sauce
1/2 t	ground cumin
1/4 cup	stir-fry sauce
1 t	ground ginger
2 cloves	garlic
1/4 cup	low-cal Italian dressing

Mix ingredients in blender. Can be used as a basting sauce.

West Texas Marinade

1/2 cup	strong coffee
1/2 cup	soy sauce
1 T	Worcestershire sauce
2 T	wine vinegar
2 cloves	garlic, minced
1 t	fine herbs

Mix all ingredients together and cover steaks several hours before cooking.

Anisette Marinade

1/4 cup	sliced green onion
2 oz.	Anisette liquor
2 T	soy sauce
3 oz.	orange juice
1/2 t	grated ginger
2 cloves	garlic, minced
1/4 t	black pepper
1/4 t	cumin

Combine all ingredients. For chops or steaks.

In Russia, moose are sometimes used as dairy animals. The milk is high in protein and fat and rich in vitamins.

STEAKS & CHOPS

Moose Fondue

Fill a fondue pot, or a small sauce pan half full of cooking oil. Cut up a couple pounds of moose tenderloin in one inch squares. Heat oil to 375°. Let everyone cook their own meat, using long forks, then dip in any of the following sauces:

Curry Sauce

1 cup	sour cream
1/4 cup	mayonnaise
1-1/2 t	curry powder
	chopped green onions

Blend all ingredients.

Horseradish Sauce

1/4 cup	butter
1/4 cup	flour
2 cups	beef broth
2-4 T	horseradish

Melt butter, add flour and whisk until smooth. Bring broth to a boil and add all at once to the flour, whisk vigorously. Simmer 5 minutes and add the horseradish.

Other sauces: mustard sauce, cáper sauce, barbecue sauce.

Marinated Moose Español

1-1/2 lbs.	moose tenderloin, cut into 6 pieces
3/4 cup	picante sauce
1/4 cup	red wine vinegar
2 or 3 cloves	garlic, minced
1 t	salt
1 t	powdered thyme
1	bay leaf
1 T	olive oil
1	medium zucchini, chopped
1	medium red bell pepper, cut in strips
1/4 t	ground cumin

Pound moose tenderloin to 1/2 inch thickness. Place in single layer in a shallow glass dish. Combine all but last 4 ingredients, mix and pour over the moose. Cover and chill overnight. Turn meat occasionally. Remove meat from marinade. Save marinade. Sauté steaks several minutes on each side. Add marinade and cook several minutes. Remove steaks from skillet, add zucchini, pepper and cumin. Cook until just tender. Spoon over moose and serve with additional picante sauce.

6 SERVINGS

Steak Chevillot

4	**moose fillets, 1-1/2 inches thick**
1/2 cup+	**red burgundy wine**
3 T	**minced onions**
1 T	**capers**
1 t	**mustard**
1 T	**flour**
3 T	**butter**

Put 1 T butter in pan, add moose and cook for 3 to 4 minutes on each side over high heat. Remove to warm serving plate. Make sauce in same pan.

SAUCE:
Cook sauce in 1 T butter with minced onions for several minutes. Add capers, then wine and cook down 'til about half, add mustard then flour premixed with remaining butter. Stir constantly, correct seasoning and serve over the steaks.

4 SERVINGS

Roulades

6 slices	bacon
4	individual moose sirloin steaks, sliced 1/3 inch thick
3 T	spicy mustard
	garlic powder
1	large onion, chopped
1 cup	water
1 can	cream of mushroom soup
1/2 t	beef bouillon

Fry or nuke bacon until crisp. Drain, then crumble. Rub steaks with garlic powder and mustard. Spread chopped onion and bacon evenly over steaks and roll up and secure with toothpicks or skewers.

Brown meat, then add water and bouillon. Cover and simmer until tender (about 1 hour). Remove from pan, add mushroom soup to pan, heat and serve over roulades.

These can be made ahead and reheated later.

4 SERVINGS

*Scaloppini Marsala**

This dish calls for veal, but I have used mini steaks that are left over when butchering.

1 lb.	moose steak odds and ends
3 oz.	butter or margarine
1/4 cup	flour
1 t	salt
4-6 oz.	marsala wine

Pound meat thin by placing between wax paper and pounding with a mallet or better yet put in a zip lock bag. Mix salt with flour and coat meat slices in mixture.

Melt butter in frying pan and brown meat quickly on each side. Add wine and cook for several minutes. Serve on warm dish with sauce from the pan.

4 SERVINGS

*From my cookbook, *Only the Best.*

Stir-fried Moose and Mushrooms

1 cup	water chestnuts
1 cup	chopped celery
1 cup	chopped peppers
1 cup	chopped onions
1/2 lb.	sliced mushrooms
3 lbs.	moose sirloin, cut in strips
1/2 t	ginger
1 T	sugar
	sherry
	olive, peanut or corn oil
	stir fry sauce or soy sauce

This dish should be cooked in a wok, but if you don't have one, a large round bottom dutch oven or even a frying pan will do.

Heat a little oil in the wok. Add the ginger and quickly sauté the veggies one at a time and remove to a bowl kept alongside the wok. A splash of sherry can be added from time to time to reduce the amount of oil used. Do the meat last and when brown return the veggies to the wok and add stir fry sauce to taste. Serve with fried or white rice or soft fried noodles.

4-6 SERVINGS

Variations

There are as many variations as there are cooks. You can replace any or all the veggies with Chinese mixed vegetables, canned water chestnuts or bamboo shoots.

The yearly harvest of moose is over 300,000 worldwide, and the herd is increasing in size!

Sukiyaki

Here we adapt the traditional Japanese dish.

3 lbs.	moose sirloin, cut in thin strips
3/4 cup	soy sauce (lo-salt)
3/4 cup	beef broth
1/4 cup	dry sherry
2 T	sugar
1 t	M.S.G. (optional)
1/2 cup	vegetable oil
1-1/2 cups	sliced onions
3/4 cups	sliced celery
1-1/4 cups	sliced mushrooms
1 cup	sliced bamboo shoots

Mix the 2nd, 3rd, 4th, 5th and 6th ingredients in a small bowl. Heat the oil in a wok or dutch oven or a deep fry pan. Add the moose and stir fry until brown. Remove to a bowl and pour half the soy sauce mixture over. Stir fry the vegetables and pour the remaining soy sauce mixture over. Add the steak, heat and serve with thin noodles. The vegetables should not be overcooked, but should be tender crisp.

6-8 SERVINGS

Steak Diane

Use good sirloin strip steaks – one for each person to be served. Recipe is given for six small steaks but can be adjusted up or down as you need.

6	**moose strip steaks**
2 T	**butter**
2 T	**olive oil**
3 T	**brandy**
2 T	**shallots or green onions**
1 t	**minced parsley**
1-10-1/2 oz.	**can, chilled consommé**
	pepper TT
1 or 2 T	**Worcestershire sauce**

Pound steaks to ¼ inch thickness using a mallet. I find that placing them in a zip-lock before pounding keeps the kitchen cleaner and you won't find pieces of meat on the ceiling. Heat butter and oil in a heavy fry pan and cook the steaks one at a time over high heat for one minute on each side. Remove to a heated platter. When all the steaks are cooked, return them to the pan, pour the brandy over and light. Shake the pan. Reduce the heat, add the shallots and cook for several minutes. Sprinkle in the parsley. Add the consommé one spoonful at a time. Remove steaks to a warm platter and keep warm. Cook the pan liquid over high heat until reduced by half. Add pepper and Worcestershire. Spoon the sauce over the steaks and serve right away. This dish loses flavor if not served piping hot. Serve with french fries or scalloped potatoes and a fresh green vegetable.

6 SERVINGS

Zegreb Sirloin Steak

Here is a recipe that I picked up in Zegreb before all the fighting began. Of course they had no moose there, but I bet they wish they had some now!

1-1/2 cups	velouté sauce (see page 36)
1/2 cup	butter or margarine
1	large onion, minced
3/4 cup	dry white wine
2-3 T	brandy
1/4 lb.	fresh mushrooms
1/2 cup	half-and-half cream
2 T	Hungarian paprika
	salt and pepper TT
6	moose sirloin steaks

Prepare velouté sauce, then melt half of the butter in a large fry pan. Add the onions and fry until tender. Don't let them burn. Pour in the wine and cook until reduced by two thirds. Pour the brandy over and ignite. Combine the sauce and the mushrooms and add to the pan. Stir in the cream, paprika and salt and pepper and heat. In another pan, melt the remaining butter and cook the steaks. Put the steaks on a heated platter and pour the sauce over. Serve with oven roasted potatoes.

6 SERVINGS

Moose Chow Mein

4 T	peanut oil
1 lb.	moose tenderloin, cut in strips
1/2 lb.	mushrooms, sliced
2 cups	celery, sliced diagonally
2	green peppers, cut in strips
2	green onions, sliced
1-1/2 cups	boiling water
3-4 t	soy sauce
	pepper TT
1 t	sugar
1-10 oz.	can Chinese vegetables
1 small jar	pimentos
1 T	corn starch
	sherry

Heat oil in wok or large fry pan. Stir fry moose a few minutes. Remove from pan. Stir fry mushrooms, celery, onions and peppers. Add boiling water and bring back to a boil for a few minutes. Remove vegetables and mix 1 T cornstarch with a little sherry and use to thicken sauce. Return to wok everything you took out plus pimento. Heat and serve with chow mein noodles.

4-5 SERVINGS

Variation
Water chestnuts and/or bamboo shoots may be added.

Moose Chops Florentine

2-10 oz.	packages frozen spinach
4	large moose loin chops
	salt
	flour
2 T	butter or margarine
2	anchovy filets, chopped
1/2 cup	chopped onions
1/2 cup	sliced mushrooms
2 t	spicy mustard
1/4 cup	red wine
1/4 cup	moose stock or bouillon

Place frozen spinach in a pot with the water and cook as directed on package. Dredge chops in salt and flour mixture and brown in a large frypan. Remove and keep warm. In the same pan heat butter, then add remaining ingredients and cook until reduced by half. Put chops back in the pan and cook until meat is cooked. Place each chop on a bed of spinach and pour the sauce over. Serve hot.

4 SERVINGS

Easy Moose and Scalloped Potatoes

Here's a quick and easy dish that you can zap in the microwave and have on the table in less than 30 minutes. This recipe is for a microwave and can, of course, be cooked in a regular oven with minor modification.

2-3 cups	moose steak cut in 1/2" cubes, cooked
1 T	butter or margarine
1/2 cup	cheese "Ritz" cracker crumbs
3 T	butter or margarine
1/2 cup	chopped celery
1/2 cup	chopped onions
2-10 oz.	packages frozen peas and potatoes (or just potatoes)
1-1/2 cups	milk
1/4 cup	chopped pimento
1 T	spicy mustard
1 T	Worcestershire sauce
1 t	nutmeg
	tomato for garnish

In a small bowl melt the 1 T of butter (30 seconds) and then mix with the crumbs. Set aside. In a 2 qt.

microwave casserole combine the 2 T of butter with the celery and onions. Cover and nuke on high for 3 minutes. Add everything but the tomato and the crumbs and cook for 12-14 minutes stirring several times while cooking. After about 10 minutes take the dish from the oven and put a slice of tomato in the center. When done remove from the oven and sprinkle the crumbs around the edge of the dish.

6 SERVINGS

The gestation period for the cow moose is from 224 to 244 days.

Korean Moose-ke-Barbe

1-1/2 lbs.	moose top round, sliced very thin
3 T	sugar or sweetener
3 T	sake
3	scallions, chopped
2 T	minced garlic
6 T	soy sauce
2 T	sesame seed oil
2 T	sesame seeds
	black pepper TT
	chopped scallions for garnish

Cut moose in bite size pieces. Dissolve the sugar in the sake and add the meat. Let stand several hours in the refrigerator. Meanwhile, combine the scallions, garlic, soy sauce, sesame oil and seeds and pepper. Add to meat and mix well. Put the moose onto long skewers and cook about 2 to 5 minutes a side. These may be done in a broiler. Garnish with the scallions. Goes well with fried rice.

4 SERVINGS

Jamaican Jerked Moose Chops

1/4 cup	olive oil
1/4 cup	wine vinegar
1/2 cup	orange juice
	juice of a fresh lime
	hot peppers TT
2 cloves	garlic, minced
6	scallions, chopped
1 T	ground allspice
3 T	chopped fresh thyme or 1 T dried
1/2 t	grated nutmeg
1/2 t	mace
1/2 t	cinnamon
	pinch of cloves
2 t	salt
1 t	black pepper
2	bay leaves
4	large moose chops, 1" thick

Mix all ingredients and pour over chops in a shallow glass bowl. Cover and marinate overnight (4 hours minimum). Turn several times. Cook on a hot grill until done to your liking. Baste liberally with the marinade. If you have any left over, boil it up and thicken it with flour and serve with the chops.

4 SERVINGS

Tenderloin with Bourbon

4-4 oz.	**moose tenderloin steaks**
1 T	**Worcestershire sauce**
1/2 cup	**bourbon**
3 T	**sour cream**
2 T	**butter or margarine**
2 T	**spicy mustard**
	pepper TT
1/2 cup	**beef broth**
1 T	**soy sauce**

Sauté the moose in the butter quickly on each side. Put soy sauce on steaks and Worcestershire sauce. Add bourbon and ignite. Transfer to a warm platter.

Add broth and mustard to skillet and heat to the boiling point. Stir a little of the sauce into the sour cream then beat the sour cream into the sauce in the pan. Do not boil. Pour over the steaks and serve hot.

4 SERVINGS

Swiss Steak

1	large round steak (2 lbs.)
	flour to dredge
3 T	oil
2 cans	consommé soup
1 cup	water
1/3 cup	ketchup
3 T	mustard
	salt and pepper
1 cup	canned stewed tomatoes
2	large onions sliced in rings
8 oz.	mushrooms
1/2	large green pepper, cut in strips
1 T	minced garlic
1/4 t	oregano
1/4 t	basil

Use an electric fry pan if you have one and heat to 400°, otherwise use a regular fry pan. Cut meat in 1 inch strips. Roll in flour and salt and pepper to taste. Brown in hot oil. Add soup and water. Stir in ketchup, mustard and tomatoes. Add onion rings. Simmer for 1 – 1½ hours. Add mushrooms, green pepper and spices. Simmer for another hour or until tender. Serve with rice or noodles.

4-6 SERVINGS

Moose and Black Bean Salsa

Here's another south of the border way to cook your moose!

1	**moose sirloin steak, cut 1-1/2" thick**
15 oz.	**can black beans, drained**
1	**large tomato, chopped**
1	**red onion, chopped**
3 T	**chopped fresh cilantro**

SEASONING MIXTURE:

1 T	**chili powder**
1 t	**ground cumin**
1 t	**salt**
1/2 t	**cayenne pepper**

Combine spices in seasoning mixture and divide in two equal parts, saving one part for salsa. Rub remaining seasoning into meat on both sides. Combine remaining ingredients and mix 'til well blended. Grill or broil meat until done to your liking. Let cool then slice across the grain. Put meat on a platter with salsa and garnish with cilantro.

6 SERVINGS

Grilled Sirloin with Stilton & Wine

Stilton is an English blue type cheese. Substitute with any blue cheese.

1-6-8 oz.	moose sirloin, each
1 pint	heavy cream
2 cups	dry white wine
1	bay leaf
6	white peppercorns
4	shallots, minced
4 oz.	Stilton cheese
	salt and pepper TT
	seedless grapes for garnish

Make a sauce by boiling together the wine, shallots, peppercorns and bay leaf. Reduce until shallots are just wet. Add cream and bring to a simmer for 5 minutes or so. Whisk in the crumbled cheese and simmer until thickened. Grill the steaks on the "barbe" and when done pour sauce over, garnish with grapes and serve with french fries and a salad.

ENOUGH SAUCE FOR 6 STEAKS

Moose Schnitzel

This is an excellent way to use those little steaks that you sometimes have when butchering.

	small moose steaks
	small moose steaks
4 T	**flour**
1	**egg, beaten**
1 cup	**fresh bread crumbs**
	salt and pepper TT
3 T	**cooking oil**
	parsley
	lemon slices

Pound steaks very thin with a mallet or rolling pin. If you put the steaks inside a zip-lock bag it will save on the clean-up. Dip the steaks in the flour, then in the egg and then into the bread crumbs. Sauté the steaks in the oil in a hot pan for a minute or so on each side. Garnish with parsley and lemon slices and serve with buttered noodles.

Schnitzel Holstein

Cook schnitzel as above and arrange on a warm

serving platter. Top each schnitzel with a fried egg and garnish the platter with anchovy filets, slices of pickled beets and dill pickles.

Paprika Schnitzel

Prepare schnitzels as above. Remove to hot platter and keep warm. Add 2 shallots, finely chopped to the butter in the pan. Cook until golden. Add 1 T of flour and 2 t of paprika, and gradually add 1 cup of hot stock and ¼ cup of cream sherry, stirring all the while. When sauce has thickened, lower flame and simmer about 5 minutes. Add ½ cup of sour cream and a little lemon juice and heat, but do not boil. Pour sauce over the meat, garnish with parsley and serve.

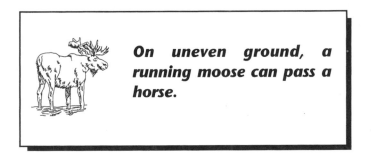

On uneven ground, a running moose can pass a horse.

ROASTS, STEWS & CASSEROLES

Braised Moose w/ Sour Cream

3 lbs.	moose stew meat
1 clove	garlic, minced
	cooking oil
1 cup	carrots, diced
1 cup	celery, diced
1 cup	onions, minced
2 t	salt
2 cups	rosé wine
3 cups	water
	A bouquet garni, parsley, bay leaves, thyme, celery tops and 6 peppercorns tied in a bag
1/4 cup	butter or margarine
4 T	flour
1-1/2 cups	heavy sour cream
2 t	paprika

Use a heavy cast iron dutch oven or a heavy kettle.

Cut meat into 2-inch cubes. Fry out garlic, then brown meat in the oil. Add vegetables and a few minutes later add the wine, water and the spices. Cover and braise the meat in a 325° oven for about 1 hour or so until meat is tender. Melt the butter in a saucepan and stir in the flour, over a low flame until sauce is thickened. Cook for a few minutes and stir in the sour cream and paprika. Put the meat and vegetables on a serving dish and pour the sauce over them. Serve with noodles, pasta or couscous.

6 SERVINGS

Burmese Ginger Moose

There are as many variations as there are cooks. You can replace any or all the veggies with Chinese mixed vegetables, canned water chestnuts or bamboo shoots.

1 cup	chopped onion
2 cloves	garlic, minced
1 t	chili powder
2 t	turmeric
2 t	ginger
2 T	soy sauce
3 lbs.	moose stew meat, cubed
6	med. fresh tomatoes or canned equivalent
	peanut oil for frying
3-4 cups	moose or beef stock

Combine first 6 ingredients in a bowl, mixing well. Add stew meat and refrigerate for 3 or 4 hours, or overnight. Heat oil in a wok or fry pan and brown stew meat. Put meat in a casserole with pan drippings, add peeled chopped tomatoes and stock. Bake covered in a 325° oven for about 3 hours or until the meat is tender. Serve with white rice.

6-8 SERVINGS

Moose and Apple Stew

1 lb.	boneless moose chuck cut
4 T	olive oil
1/2 cup	chopped onions
1-10-1/2 oz.	can beef broth
3 cups	apple cider
1/2 t	thyme
3	bay leaves
	salt and pepper TT
1/2 lb.	carrots, cut
4	apples, cored and chopped
3 T	A-1 sauce
	flour or cornstarch to thicken
	water or cider as needed

Brown meat in oil. Add onions, broth, cider and seasonings. Cover and bring to a boil. Simmer about 1¼ hours or until meat is starting to become tender. Add carrots and cook 15 more minutes. Add apples and cook for a few minutes. Thicken with flour or cornstarch. Correct seasoning. Serve with boiled potatoes or rice.

4 SERVINGS

Moose Bourguignonne

Here is a french stew that seems made for moose meat!

1/4 lb.	bacon, chopped
2 T	olive oil
2 T	flour
1 t	salt
	pepper TT
1/2 t	paprika
2 lbs.	boneless moose chuck, cubed
1/2 cup	sliced onions
2-3 cups	moose or beef stock or bouillon
1-1/2 cups	burgundy
4 T	tomato paste
2 cloves	garlic, minced
1	bouquet garni (a mixture of bay leaf, parsley, thyme and marjoram)
12	small onions or 24 pearl onions

Sauté bacon in olive oil. Remove to a large casserole. Mix flour, salt and pepper and dredge the moose cubes. Place in the fry pan with the sliced onions and paprika and sauté until brown. Place in casserole. Pour 2 cups of the stock and the burgundy in the fry pan. Add the tomato paste and garlic. Bring to a boil and pour over meat in the casserole. Add enough stock to cover and bake in a 325° oven until meat is tender, anywhere from 1-3 1/2 hours. While this is cooking, boil onions in salted water until almost tender, then drain. Cook the mushrooms in butter until golden. Add vegetables to the casserole when the meat is tender. Cook a few minutes. Correct seasoning and thicken slightly with cornstarch or flour if needed. Serve with buttered noodles.

6 SERVINGS

Moose eat twigs, leaves and water plants.

Moose with English Walnuts

3 lbs.	lean moose meat
24	pearl onions
1 cup	red wine
1 T	parsley
2 cloves	garlic, mashed
	salt and pepper TT
1 cup	walnuts
2 t	orange rind, shredded
3 T	oil
5-6 t	flour
1/2 t	thyme
2	bay leaves
2-3 cups	moose stock, or bouillon
3 cups	celery, sliced
2-3 oz.	sherry

Use a dutch oven and brown the meat in the oil. Remove meat and cook onions in the same pot until golden. Add 2 T flour and brown. Add wine and stock or bouillon. Next comes all the spices (not the orange rind). Return the meat to the pot and cook for 1 hour. Add the celery and walnuts and cook for another hour. Thicken to the desired consistency and just before serving, sprinkle the orange rind over the stew and serve over noodles or rice.

SERVES A BUNCH

Moose with Noodles, Sheffield

3 lbs.	moose stew meat
	flour to dredge
	salt and pepper TT
1 t	freshly grated nutmeg
1 cup	onions, chopped fine
1/2 t	thyme
1/2 cup	carrots, grated
3/4 cup	dry red wine
1 cup	moose stock or beef broth
1 t	tarragon
3-4 T	bacon drippings or oil
	noodles
1 t	poppy seeds

Cut the stew meat in 1-inch cubes and dredge in the flour mixed with nutmeg. Brown in a large skillet in bacon drippings. Add onions, carrots and cover. Cook until browned. Add wine, broth and spices. Cover and cook over low heat for at least 1 1/2 hours, until the meat is very tender. Add more broth if needed. Boil up some noodles, drain and return to the pot with a good hunk of butter. Throw in a t of poppy seeds and heat. Serve the moose over the noodles.

6 SERVINGS

Pot Roast with Prunes

4 lbs.	chuck or rump roast
4 T	fat or oil
3	large onions, sliced
2 cloves	garlic, minced
1/2 lb.	uncooked seeded prunes
4	cloves
	salt and pepper TT
2 cup	cider

Brown meat in hot fat. Add onions and garlic and cook 'til onions are brown. Add remaining ingredients, lower heat, cover and simmer slowly until tender – up to 3 or 4 hours depending on the toughness of the meat. If more liquid is needed add a little water.

Serve with buttered noodles.

6-8 SERVINGS

Moose, Indonesian Style

The original recipe calls for pork, but I have used venison and moose meat with much success.

2 lbs.	moose meat, cubed
1 cup	peanut butter
1 T	coriander seed, crushed
2 cloves	garlic, crushed
1-1/2 cups	chopped onion
2 T	lemon juice
3 T	honey
5 T	soy sauce
1/2 cup	chicken bouillon

Mix all ingredients except moose meat in a large saucepan or skillet and bring to a boil. Simmer sauce 15 minutes then add cubed meat and cook 'til done. Serve with white rice.

4-6 SERVINGS

Variation

Half a cup of chopped peanuts can be added to the rice while cooking.

Moose Stroganoff

Plenty of "meese" (that's plural for moose in the Hunyak language) grow in Russia. This is the way I would cook them if I lived over there.

3 T	flour
1 t	salt
	freshly ground pepper
1-1/2 lbs.	moose sirloin steak, cut in 2 x 1/2" strips
6 T	butter
1/2 cup	chopped shallots*
1/2 lb.	sliced mushrooms
1 clove	garlic, pressed
1/2 cup	cream sherry
1 cup	moose or beef stock or bouillon
1 t	chervil
1/4 t	paprika
3/4 cup	sour cream

* Mild onions may be used.

Heat half of the butter in a pan. Dredge meat with flour mixed with the spices. Add meat to the pan and cook rare. Remove meat from the pan, add the remaining butter and then add mushrooms, garlic and shallots. Cook until tender but not brown. Return meat to the pan and add sherry, bouillon, chervil and paprika. Reduce until liquid is reduced by half then add the sour cream. Simmer and do not let boil for a few minutes. Serve over rice with broiled tomatoes.

6 SERVINGS

Variations

1. Add 2 T spicy mustard near the end of the cooking.
2. A little ketchup or tomato sauce can be added.
3. From Donna Wall, North Bay: 1 oz. brandy and 1 T lemon juice to the above.

Alaskan Chuck Roast

5-6 lb.	moose chuck roast
2	large peppers, chopped
4	large onions, chopped
1 t	instant beef bouillon
1 t	black pepper
2 cloves	garlic, minced or pressed
2 bottles	ketchup (20 oz.)
1/2 cup	sugar
1 t	chili powder
10	whole cloves
1 t	dry mustard
1 t	cinnamon
1 t	allspice
2	bay leaves
2-4 T	Worcestershire sauce
1 cup	cider vinegar
1 t	ginger

Mix all ingredients. Put meat in a pan that can be covered and pour sauce over moose. Cover tightly and cook in a slack oven (225-250°) for 6-6½ hours. Slice or shred with two forks. Can be served on sandwiches or over rice.

6-10 SERVINGS

Moose-Ham Casserole

A good way to use leftover moose steak!

1	**medium head of cauliflower**
1 cup	**chopped cooked ham**
1 cup	**chopped cooked moose steak**
1/4 lb.	**small fresh mushrooms**
4 T	**butter or margarine**
1/3 cup	**all purpose flour**
1 cup	**milk**
4 oz.	**sharp cheddar cheese**
1/2 cup	**sour cream**
2 T	**fresh dill or 1 T dried**
1 cup	**soft bread crumbs**
	grated parmesan cheese

Break cauliflower into buds. Cook in boiling salted water and cook 10 minutes or so until tender. Drain. Sauté mushrooms, ham and moose in the butter, stir in flour. Add milk all at once and stir until the mixture thickens. Add cheddar cheese, sour cream and dill, chopped fine.

Mix the whole mess together and dump into a greased 2 qt. casserole. Sprinkle with the parmesan cheese and bake in 350° oven until piping hot. About 45-50 minutes.

6 SERVINGS

Sicilian Pot Roast

3 to 6 lb.	moose chuck roast
	slivered garlic
	sliced black olives
	salt and pepper TT
3 t	oil
	bouquet garni
1 can	tomato soup
1 cup	white wine
4-5	large onions, quartered
1/2 lb.	mushrooms, sliced
	water if needed
	flour to thicken gravy

Cut slits in meat and insert garlic and olives through the roast. Heat oil and brown meat in a dutch oven or a large pot. Add soup, wine, salt and pepper. Cover and cook 2 to 3 hours until tender. Add onions and mushrooms and liquid if needed. Cook another 20 minutes. Correct seasoning and serve.

10-12 SERVINGS

Roast Moose w/ Poivrade Sauce

Prepare a 4-5 lb. moose roast for the oven. Rub with garlic and soy sauce and cover the roast with bacon slices. Roast in a 450° oven for 30 minutes. Reduce the oven temperature to 400° and cook until done. Use an oven thermometer and when it reads just below beef rare take it out of the oven. Pour off the fat but leave the pan juices. Add a couple of oz. of cognac to the pan and ignite. Stir and mix with pan juices. Mix with Poivrade sauce and serve with the moose. Goes good with oven roasted potatoes and a green vegetable.

10 SERVINGS

Variations

The above roast can be served with many sauces, and some of the best are hunter, mustard, Cumberland, cranberry and bearnaise sauces. Also try mushroom, horseradish and curry sauce, which are all listed in the sauce section.

Roast Moose with Pecans and Apples

5-6 lbs.	**moose roast**
	mint jelly
	salt and pepper
1 cup	**chopped pecans**
1 cup	**chopped apples**
	apple cider or wine

Rub salt and pepper over meat. Make a cavity in the meat and rub inside and out with mint jelly. Stuff cavity with the apples and pecans. Cover roast with suet and tie with string. Place moose in an oven pan and put cider (about a cup) in the bottom. Seal the pan with foil. Bake at 350° 'til done (beef rare on a meat thermometer). Make a gravy from the pan drippings.

8-10 SERVINGS

Roast Saddle of Moose

	saddle or any good roast of moose
	any of the marinades (see page 85)
	soy sauce
	garlic powder
6 slices	of bacon
1 cup	onions slivered
2 oz.	rosé wine
	foil

Make marinade and put meat in it for at least 6 hours, preferably overnight. Lay in large foil (It should be large enough to enclose meat. If you don't have large enough foil, splice two pieces together by folding several times). Rub meat with soy sauce and garlic powder. Cover with the onions and put bacon on top. Add the wine and seal the foil. Bake in a 350° oven 'til done (about 15 minutes per lb. or until a meat thermometer registers beef rare). Remember meat will continue to cook for a while after you take it from the oven. Serve with Cumberland sauce.

SERVINGS DEPEND ON THE SIZE OF THE ROAST

RIBS & KEBABS

Braised Short Ribs

3 lbs.	moose short ribs
1/2 cup	flour
2 t	instant beef bouillon
	freshly ground black pepper
3 T	bacon fat or oil
4	onions, chopped
1/2 cup	chili sauce
1 small can	crushed pineapple
1 T	brown sugar
1 cup	water

Dredge ribs in flour and brown in hot fat. Add remaining ingredients. Cover tightly and cook until done. You may need to add a little water from time to time. Requires about 2 1/2 hours' cooking time.

4-6 SERVINGS

Moose Kebabs

This dish is better if the meat is marinated overnight in the refrigerator.

3 lbs.	moose chuck, cubed 1-1/2"
1 cup	dry white wine
1/2 cup	lemon juice
1/4 cup	olive oil
2 cloves	garlic, mashed
1 t	oregano
1/2 t	thyme
1/4 t	basil
3 T	Worcestershire sauce
	salt or soy sauce and pepper TT

Combine above ingredients in a bowl and add the moose chunks. Marinate at least four hours.

Depending what you have on hand or what you like most, use any of the following fruits or vegetables.

white or Vidalia onions	fresh pineapple
green or red peppers	apples, halved
large mushrooms	kumquats
small firm tomatoes	

Halve onions and tomatoes and alternate whatever you are using with moose chunks that are well drained. Reserve the marinade for a basting sauce. Run through with long skewers and grill on the "barbe" about 15 minutes, brushing with the marinade frequently. Serve with rice or couscous.

8 SERVINGS

The cows give birth to one or two calves, rarely three.

ORGAN MEATS

Boiled Moose Heart

The heart is perhaps the tastiest part of the moose, and seldom returns with the hunter, having been eaten at the hunting lodge or camp.

The heart is placed in a pot and covered with water. Salt and pepper are really all that is needed, but you can add a chopped up onion and maybe a few bay leaves if you like. Boil until the heart is tender and cooked through. Remove from the pot and slice. Make sandwiches with dark rye bread. For condiments use horseradish, spicy mustard and mayonnaise. Add a slice of onion or some chutney if you like.

Rolled Moose Heart, Stuffed

Cut into outer wall of heart with a sharp knife and cut around heart, continuing until you have a long strip, sort of like paring an apple.

Brown meat quickly on both sides and remove from heat.

Stuffings

You can use your favorite stuffing or one of the ones below:
1. 1 cup soft bread crumbs, 2 T melted butter, salt and pepper TT, 1/2 cup chopped apples. Moisten with sherry.
2. Use mushrooms in place of apples in the above recipe.
3. Use raisins or prunes instead of apples.
4. Use sausage instead of the above.
5. Use cooked rice in place of bread crumbs.
6. Make with wild rice instead of white rice.
7. Add some chopped onion to any of the above.

Stuff heart, then wrap with bacon. Hold with toothpicks, then put in a covered casserole. Add a little wine and bake at 325° for 45-55 minutes.

4 SERVINGS

Tongue

Cover tongue with water, add salt, 1 t per quart of water. Add a sliced onion, a clove of garlic chopped, a few peppercorns, a t of thyme and cook 'til tender, up to 3 1/2 hours. Serve with horseradish sauce.

Sweet and Sour Tongue

2 T	butter or margarine
2 T	flour
1/2 t	salt
1/4 t	pepper
1 cup	tongue stock or bouillon
2 T	sugar
2 T	vinegar
8 slices	cooked tongue

Blend butter, flour and seasonings. Add stock and cook until thickened. Add remaining ingredients. Cook for about 5 minutes. Serve with fried rice or regular white rice.

4 SERVINGS

Tongue in Raisin Sauce

3/4 cup	brown sugar
3 T	cornstarch
1-1/2 cups	broth from tongue or bouillon
1/4 cup	vinegar
1/2 cup	raisins
1	lemon, sliced thin
1 T	oil or bacon fat

Mix all ingredients in top of double boiler and cook until raisins are plump. Stir occasionally. Serve over hot tongue slices.

DESSERT

Chocolate Mousse (Moose)

4	egg yolks
3/4 cup	confectioners sugar
1/4 cup	orange liqueur
6 oz.	semi-sweet chocolate
4 T	strong coffee
6 oz.	softened, unsalted butter
1/2 cup	diced, glazed orange peel
4	egg whites
	pinch of salt
1 T	granulated sugar
2 cups	whipped cream

Beat the egg yolks and sugar together in a stainless steel mixing bowl until mixture is pale yellow. Beat in the orange liqueur. Set bowl over very hot water and continue beating for 3 to 4 minutes until foamy and too hot to the touch. Then beat over cold water for another 3 to 4 minutes until mixture is cool and has the consistency of mayonnaise.

Melt chocolate and coffee over hot water. Remove from heat and beat in butter a little at a time. Beat chocolate into the egg yolk mixture then the orange peel.

Beat the egg whites and salt until soft peaks are formed. Sprinkle in sugar and beat until stiff peaks are formed. Stir $1/4$ of the whites into the chocolate mixture and fold in the rest.

Put into individual dessert cups and refrigerate for 2 hours. Serve with whipped cream.

6-8 SERVINGS

Appendix

Subject	Page
Standard Measure Conversions	152
Oven Temperatures	154
Moose Hunt and Freezer Inventory	155

Standard Measure Conversions

Weight (Gram Measure)

no. of grams (g) = no. of ounces x 28
no. of kilograms (Kg) = no. of pounds x 0.45
1 Kg = 1000 g
30 g = 1 ounce
100 g = 1/4 lb.
250 g = 1/2 lb.
500 g = 1 lb.
1 Kg = 2 lb.

Small Measure

1 mL = 1/4 tsp.
2 mL = 1/2 tsp.
5 mL = 1 tsp.
15 mL = 1 tbsp.
30 mL = 2 tbsp.
45 mL = 3 tbsp.

Dry & Liquid Measure

millilitres (mL) = no. of ounces x 30*
no. of litres (L) = no. of quarts x 0.95
1000 mL = 1 L
60 mL = 1/4 cup
75 mL = 1/3 cup
75 mL = 1/2 cup
175 mL = 3/4 cup
250 mL = 1 cup
1 L = 4 cups

*Use this conversion to obtain the approximate size of baking pan needed for metric recipe.

Oven Temperatures

Range	°C	°F	°Gas Mark
Very cool	110	225	1/4
	120	250	1/2
Cool	140	275	1
	150	300	2
Moderate	160	325	3
	180	350	4
Moderately hot	190	375	5
	200	400	6
Hot	220	425	7
	230	450	8
Very hot	240	475	9

Moose Hunt

Date: _____   Area Hunted: _____

Guide: _____   Address: _____

_____

No. Days Hunted: _____   Moose Sightings: _____

Members in Hunting Party: _____

_____

Results: Bulls _____   Cows _____   Racks _____

Expenses: Licence Fee _____   Guide _____

Transportation _____   Food _____   Booze_____

Tips_____   Butchering_____   Other_____

Butchering: Weight of 4 quarters _____

Estimated Live Weight _____   Weight of Meat _____

Freezer Packages:

_____Roasts: _____

_____Steaks: _____

_____Chops: _____

_____Hamburg: _____

_____Stew: _____

_____Other:_____

Use the above freezer inventory to keep an accurate count
of meat remaining. Put a hash mark (/) after proper
category when you remove a package from the freezer.
Enter your total packages of each before that entry.

Moose Hunt

Date: _____ Area Hunted: _____

Guide: _____ Address: _____

_____

No. Days Hunted: _____ Moose Sightings: _____

Members in Hunting Party: _____

_____

Results: Bulls _____   Cows _____   Racks_____

Expenses: Licence Fee _____   Guide _____

Transportation _____ Food _____ Booze_____

Tips_____ Butchering_____ Other_____

Butchering: Weight of 4 quarters _____

Estimated Live Weight _____ Weight of Meat _____

Freezer Packages:

_____Roasts: _____

_____Steaks: _____

_____Chops: _____

_____Hamburg: _____

_____Stew: _____

_____Other:_____

Use the above freezer inventory to keep an accurate count
of meat remaining. Put a hash mark (/) after proper
category when you remove a package from the freezer.
Enter your total packages of each before that entry.

Moose Hunt

Date: _____ Area Hunted: _____

Guide: _____ Address: _____

_____

No. Days Hunted: _____ Moose Sightings: _____

Members in Hunting Party: _____

_____

Results: Bulls _____ Cows _____ Racks _____

Expenses: Licence Fee _____ Guide _____

Transportation _____ Food _____ Booze _____

Tips _____ Butchering _____ Other _____

Butchering: Weight of 4 quarters _____

Estimated Live Weight _____ Weight of Meat _____

Freezer Packages:

_____ Roasts: _____

_____ Steaks: _____

_____ Chops: _____

_____ Hamburg: _____

_____ Stew: _____

_____ Other: _____

Use the above freezer inventory to keep an accurate count
of meat remaining. Put a hash mark (/) after proper
category when you remove a package from the freezer.
Enter your total packages of each before that entry.

Index

A

Alaska Chuck Roast, 130
Anisette Marinade, 92

B

Barbecue Sauce, 21
Bearnaise Sauce, 19
Bechamel Sauce, 18
Beer Sauce, 22

C

Caper Marinade, 90
Caper Sauce, 25
Casseroles and Pies, 117
Cider and Raisin Sauce, 24
Colonel's Game Sauce, 26
Cooked Marinade, 87
Corned Moose and Parsnips, 51
Cornish Pasty, 76

Cranberry Meat Loaf, 80
Cranberry-Orange Sauce, 24
Crock Pots, 9
Crock Pot Moose Soup, 9
Cumberland Sauce, 27
Currant Glaze, 30
Curried Moose w/ Eggplant, 65
Curry Sauce, 28

D

Dessert, 147
Dill Sauce, 29
Double Consommé, 4
Drawn Butter Sauce, 23

E

Easy Moose and Scalloped
    Potatoes, 107
Eggplant, 65

F

Fayaway Meat Loaf, 78
Fettucini Bolognese, 72
French Canadian Moose Pie, 83

G

Great Southwestern Soup, 10
Grilled Sirloin w/ Stilton and
    Wine, 114

H

Hamburg, 57
Home Cured Pastrami, 54
Honey Glaze, 30
Horseradish Cream Dressing, 31
How to Corn Moose Meat, 47

I

Inners, 141

J

Jamaican Jerked Moose Chops, 110
Jellied Wine Consommé, 5

K

Korean Moose-Ke-Barbe, 109

L

Low-Cal Marinade, 91

M

Madeira Consommé, 5
Madeira Sauce, 32
Marina Cay Casserole, 84
Meat Loaf in a Blanket, 81
Mexicali Stuffed Peppers, 75
Moose and Apple Stew, 121
Moose and Barley Soup, 13
Moose and Black Bean Salsa, 113
Mooseballs with Lemon Sauce, 60
Moose, Beans and Bourbon, 77
Moose Chili Con Carne, 68
Moose Chow Mein, 105
Moose Fondue, 94
Moose Ham Casserole, 131
Moose Indonesian Style, 127
Moose Kebabs, 139
Moose Manicotti, 66
Moose Meatballs w/Prunes, 74
Moose Meat Roll, 63
Moose Mincemeat, 67
Moose-saka, 70
Moose Sausage, 37
Moose Schnitzel, 115
Moose Stroganoff, 128
Moose w/ English Walnuts, 124
Moose with Noodles, Sheffield,
    125

Moscovite Sauce, 32
Mushroom Consommé, 4
Mushroom Sauce, 33
Mustard Glaze, 30
Mustard Sauce, 23

N

Norwegian Vegetable Soup, 12

O

Oriental Marinade, 90

P

Paprika Schnitzel, 116
Poivrade Sauce, 34
Pot-au-Feu, 8
Pot Roast with Prunes, 126

R

Red Wine Sauce, 35
Romaine Sauce, 35
Roulades, 97
Roasts, 117
Roast Moose w/ Pecans and
    Apples, 134
Roast Moose w/ Poivrade Sauce,
    133
Roast Saddle of Moose, 135

S

Sandwiches, 130, 142
Sauerbraten, 56
Sauces, 15
Sausage, 37
Sausage with Polenta, 42
Scaloppini Marsala, 98
Schnitzel Holstein, 115
Sicilian Pot Roast, 132
Spanish Rice, 73
Steak Diane, 102
Stuffed Peppers, 62
Sukiyaki, 101
Surf and Turf Pasta, 61
Sweet and Sour Tongue, 144

T

Tomato Glaze, 30
Tongue, 144
Tongue in Raisin Sauce, 145

W

West Texas Marinade, 91
White Roux, 17

Z

Zebreb Sirloin Steak, 104

About the Author

John J. (Jack) Koneazny was born in Hartford, Connecticut. He served in the U.S. Martime Service and the U.S. Army during World War II, having severed two years in the European theater of operations. He spend 28 years in the Army Reserves and worked as a tree surgeon until his retirement.

Jack and his wife Dottie travelled extensively on their Bahama-built sailboat "Fayaway" for almost 20 winters and have travelled throughout Europe and the Caribbean since their retirement.

They spend their winters in Key Largo, Florida and their summers in the Berkshires of Massachusetts.

Colonel Koneazny and his wife published their cookbook *Only the Best* in 1993. He is also the author of *Signal Hoists for Yachtsmen* and numerous magazine articles on cooking, boating and gardening. He is working on several other books at this time and is food editor for *The Boating World*. Recently, his newest work was published, *Behind Friendly Lines: Tales from World War II*.

For more copies of
The Moose Cookbook
contact General Store Publishing House
499, O'Brien Road,
Renfrew, Ontario
K7V 4A6
(613) 432-7697 or 1-800-465-6072
or Fax (613) 432-7184
www.gsph.com

A TASTE OF CANADA SERIES

Cooking For One $8.95
The Chicken Little Cookbook $8.95
Cheese Cheese.. $8.95
The Little Gourmet Gas Barbecue Cookbook........... $8.95
Back to the Grind... $8.95

MORE COOKBOOKS

Maria Elena's Mexican Cuisine $17.95
Yeast-Free Feast $14.95

ALSO BY COLONEL JOHN J. KONEAZNY
Behind Friendly Lines:
Tales from World War II $24.95